DISCARD

UNDERSTANDING
MEMES
AND
INTERNET
SATIRE

Jeff Mapua

E Enslow Publishing

101 W. 23rd Street
Suite 240
New York, NY 10011
USA

enslow.com

Published in 2019 by Enslow Publishing, LLC.
101 W. 23rd Street, Suite 240, New York, NY 10011

Copyright © 2019 by Enslow Publishing, LLC.

Cataloging-in-Publication Data

Names: Mapua, Jeff.
Title: Understanding memes and internet satire / Jeff Mapua.
Description: New York : Enslow Publishing, 2019. | Series: Critical thinking about digital media | Includes bibliographic references and index.
Identifiers: ISBN 9781978505698 (pbk.) | ISBN 9781978504745 (library bound)
Subjects: LCSH: Digital media—Social aspects. | Internet—Social aspects. | Memes.
Classification: LCC HM851.M3868 2019 | DDC 302.23/1—dc23

Printed in the United States of America

To Our Readers: We have done our best to make sure all website addresses in this book were active and appropriate when we went to press. However, the author and the publisher have no control over and assume no liability for the material available on those websites or on any websites they may link to. Any comments or suggestions can be sent by email to customerservice@enslow.com.

Photo Credits: Cover, p. 1 (silhouette) Buena Vista Images/Photodisc/Getty Images; cover, p. 1 (background) Neilson Barnard/Getty Images; p. 5 Kyle T Perry/Shutterstock.com; p. 9 Michael K. McDermott/Shutterstock.com; p. 11 Taylor Hill/Getty Images; p. 13 molekuul_be/Shutterstock.com; p. 18 Rawpixel.com/Shutterstock.com; p. 20 Redpixel.pl/Shutterstock.com; p. 22 © AP Images; p. 25 Ole Lukoje/Shutterstock.com; p. 29 Annette Shaff/Shutterstock.com; p. 31 Rainer_81/Shutterstock.com; p. 36 Alex Malikov/Shutterstock.com; p. 39 DEA/A. Dagli Orti/De Agostini/Getty Images; p. 41 AF archive/Alamy Stock Photo; p. 44 CBS Photo Archive/Getty Images; p. 48 OneSmallSquare/Shutterstock.com; p. 50 Christos Georghiou/Shutterstock.com; p. 52 Yevgen Chornobay/Shutterstock.com; p. 57 Marzufello/Shutterstock.com; p. 59 dennizn/Shutterstock.com; p. 62 Frederic Legrand COMEO/Shutterstock.com; lightbulb icon okili77/Shutterstock.com.

CONTENTS

INTRODUCTION

Tide, a Procter & Gamble company known for making laundry detergent, introduced a new product in 2012 to help people wash clothes. Called a Tide Pod, the product was a small packet containing heavily concentrated laundry detergent that dissolves in water. The packets look suspiciously like candy and initially gained national attention when young children mistakenly tried to eat them.[1]

Many people noticed how the detergent packets' design resembled food. The satire website the *Onion* posted an article poking fun at the Tide Pod, jokingly claiming that the company would soon release a sour apple flavor version. Their humor post included a supposed quote from a Tide spokeswoman claiming that the new version featured a multi-chamber design to keep "the key ingredients of detergent, color protector, and a bubble gum center" separated.[2] Chefs and bakers even jumped onto the trend by designing donuts and pizzas to look like Tide Pods.[3]

However, at some point, older children began eating the detergent packets. Similar to other "challenges" that

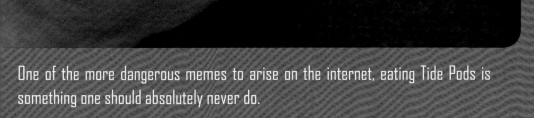

One of the more dangerous memes to arise on the internet, eating Tide Pods is something one should absolutely never do.

became popular among teenagers, such as the "cinnamon challenge," where the objective was to eat a spoonful of cinnamon without drinking anything, the Tide pod challenge dared people to upload a video of themselves eating the detergent onto the internet. The challenge spread online, and an increasing number of teenagers were poisoning themselves for seemingly no reason. In 2017, almost 220 teenagers were exposed to the detergent packets. This was in addition to more than 10,500 children five years old or younger were similar cases.[4]

Ingesting a laundry detergent packet can cause health problems including a change in blood pressure and heart rate, losing consciousness, or even seizures. The liquid can cause people to aspirate if it is inhaled into the lungs. The risks are even higher for those with other medical conditions such as asthma.[5]

Many blame the media coverage for making the Tide Pod challenge popular. However, Claire McCarthy, MD, a faculty editor at Harvard Health Publications, believes that the adolescent brain is also at fault for teens risking death. She points out that adolescence is the time in a person's life when the brain transitions from childhood to adulthood. Children are able to learn quickly from a large amount of information, while adults have connections in the brain that allow them to work more quickly and effectively. Adolescents, however, have yet to build connections to the part of the brain known as the frontal lobe. This is where the brain controls insight, judgment, and risk-taking behaviors. Essentially, teens are more likely to take risks because their brains have not yet learned to properly judge a situation.[6]

McCarthy explains how social media pressures take advantage of teens' risk-taking natures. There are hundreds, and potentially millions, of people online daring teens to take a challenge. In the first three weeks of 2018, the American Association of Poison Control Centers reported eighty-six cases of intentional exposure to laundry detergent packets.[7] What began as something perfect for internet satire grew into a full-blown trend, or what we now know as a meme.

THE SELFISH MEME

Although they seem to be everywhere on the internet today, memes are still a mystery to many people. Not everyone knows exactly what a meme is or even how it is pronounced. People label many things online as a meme when they are not, or they participate in spreading a meme without even knowing it. Defining memes can help understand what they are and how they have become so popular on the internet.

What Is a Meme?

The word "meme" was first used in the 1976 book called *The Selfish Gene* by an Oxford biologist named Richard Dawkins. In his book, Dawkins explains the mechanics of evolution. He defines genes as DNA molecules. Genes can express themselves in plants and animals in different ways. For example, one gene could give a person brown eyes or influence height. Dawkins states that genes only have one goal of replicating, or making copies of, themselves. Animals, plants, and all living things can be seen as a collection of genes, and the one goal is to make copies of themselves. In people, genes are replicated when they have children. A parent's genes live on in their children. Dogs' genes are replicated when they have puppies, and so on.[1] Genes are considered "selfish" because they do anything to make copies of themselves.

Over time, genes adapt and join with others to help replicate. Giraffes with the longest necks are able to reach the leaves on the highest tree branches, giving them an edge in survival over giraffes with shorter necks. So these giraffes,

The length of giraffes' necks is a common example of gene adaptation. Biologist Richard Dawkins argues that culture evolves over time just as genes do.

specifically those with genes that give giraffes longer necks, have a better chance of survival while short-necked giraffes and their genes are phased out over long periods of time.

Dawkins goes on to explain that human culture evolves over time, too. He uses language as an example. Someone who spoke English hundreds of years ago would have a hard time speaking with someone who speaks English today. There would be words that the other person did not know the meaning of, and even the accents may pose a problem in understanding. Language has evolved over the years.

But how could this be? There are no DNA molecules that pass on language. Dawkins proposes that something else is replicating itself and being passed down through younger generations. Instead of DNA, this new replicator passes on what Dawkins calls "a unit of cultural transmission, or a unit of imitation." The word "imitation" comes from the Greek *mimeme*, and Dawkins shortens this to be simply "meme." This also resembles *même*, the French word for memory. "Meme" is pronounced to rhyme with "cream."[2]

Memetics is the study of how memes work, interact, replicate, and evolve. Scientists and biologists see memes as the secret code of human behavior. They can help people understand how religion, politics, and more evolve in human culture. Instead of seeing culture through the eyes of people or society, it is instead described from the point of view of the meme. A scientist who studies thought and mental organization describes memes as ideas, while a psychologist may describe a meme as a unit of cultural heredity.[3]

Richard Dawkins

Professor Richard Dawkins was born in 1941. He went to the University of Oxford in England, where he earned a degree in zoology and an MA and PhD. He was an assistant professor of zoology at the University of California, Berkeley for two years before moving back to the United Kingdom to be a lecturer at Oxford.

Dawkins became the first to hold the Simonyi Professorship for the Public Understanding of Science. Serving from 1995 to 2008, his goal was to make science more accessible to a wider audience.

He is most well known for his work in evolution and natural selection. In addition to *The Selfish Gene*, he has written other books including *The Blind Watchmaker* and *The God Delusion*.[4]

Richard Dawkins is responsible for coining the term "meme" in 1976 in his book *The Selfish Gene*.

Types of Memes

Memes were originally defined as "units of cultural transmission" or a "unit of imitation." Memes can be understood in terms of culture, but there are more concrete examples of memes to help one understand the concept better.

One way to see memes is as an idea. Jacques Monod is a biologist from Paris and winner of the Nobel Prize in 1965 for his work with ribonucleic acid, or RNA, and how it transfers genetic information.

He imagined that the world of living organisms, or biosphere, was a level above nonliving matter. He further imagined an "abstract kingdom" that is a level above the biosphere. In this "kingdom" live ideas that Monod believed could "cause ideas and help evolve new ideas." This is one way to think about what memes are.[5]

Memes compete for people's attention and jump from a person's brain to another person's brain by imitation. Ideas can arise or reappear, and they can slowly fade and disappear forever. One idea that Dawkins points out is a belief in God. It is an idea that has been around for thousands of years and replicates in words, music, and art. Another example is the idea that Earth orbits the Sun. It competes with other ideas to survive. Being true may help a meme survive, but it is just one of many factors that keep an idea around.[6]

A meme can also be a catchphrase. A catchphrase is a well-known sentence, phrase, word, or expression that is used repeatedly. Some have been around for many years and can spread through print, music, or other media. There are many

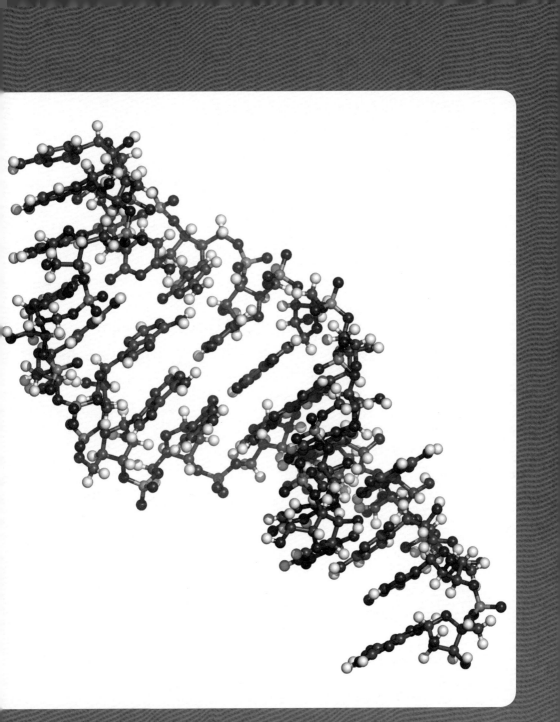

Jacques Monod, known for his work with RNA (seen here), imagined a series of kingdoms in the biological world sharing information and spawning new ideas, just as memes do.

examples of catchphrases throughout history such as "May the Force be with you" from the *Star Wars* movie franchise, and "Dilly dilly!" from a Bud Light marketing campaign. A catchphrase can change, or mutate, over time, too. The catchphrase "survival of the fittest" has mutated into various forms such as "survival of the fattest" and "survival of the twittest."[7]

One of the more popular types of memes today are images. Famous paintings such as the *Mona Lisa* (remixed to involve some form of pop culture) are some of the strongest types of memes. These memes endure without necessarily existing in physical reality; many involve aliens or monsters. A tour guide at the Metropolitan Museum of Art once said about a portrait of George Washington, "This may not be what [he] looked like then, but this is what he looks like now."[8]

Memes can also be fashion, clothes, and how to accomplish a task. While there are many types of memes, it is important to point out what memes are not. Objects are not memes. So while the actual *Mona Lisa* painting itself is not a meme, the image of her inside people's heads is a meme. Objects can instead be considered a meme vehicle. One way to think about it is that a dancer is not a meme, the dance itself is.[9]

Imitation Game

Memes replicate themselves by moving from one person's brain to another. Professor Dawkins calls this process imitation. For example, a student hears or reads about a good idea and passes it onto her friends and family. If the idea catches on, it can propagate, or spread and promote, itself over a wide area. Some memes are better than others at replication or imitation.[10]

The qualities of a meme that determine how successful it can be in survival are longevity, the ability to reproduce many copies and the ability to make high-quality copies. Compared to the other two qualities, longevity is not as vital to a meme's success. Of course, the longer a particular copy of a meme, or how long it remains in a person's thoughts, increases its chances to copy itself into another person's mind.[11]

The ability to reproduce many copies depends on a meme's acceptability or popularity. For example, a song that many people find memorable or catchy has a better chance of surviving over time than a forgettable song with a boring melody. However, while some memes are great at reproducing itself many times over in a short period of time, they can quickly disappear. Memes like these include fashion trends that come and go.[12]

The copies a meme makes of itself must be of high quality, meaning it can distinguish itself from others like it. However, as anyone who has ever played the telephone game knows, it is hard to spread the same idea among many people without it changing. A meme, Dawkins explains, is the smallest fragment of an idea that can still be "sufficiently distinctive and memorable." For example, this could be just a small section of a song that, when people hear it, can recognize what song it is. Only these small pieces must be copied well.[13]

Live Transmission

For much of human history, memes' main mode of transmission was word of mouth. Eventually they were able to spread through writing and then print. Today, memes are spread through the most transformative communications tool humans have thus far experienced: the internet. People can easily copy, paste, and share memes with anyone with an internet connection.[14]

Dawkins himself saw the power computers could have in spreading memes. Before computers were common in every household, he saw that memes and information could be passed from one computer to another on discs. He even jumped ahead and predicted that networks of computers would be perfect for "self-replicating programs to flourish."[15]

Memes on the Internet

With so many aspects of daily life moving online, such as shopping and reading the news, communication is often now done through the internet. It is how people pass on thoughts and ideas to others, making it a perfect tool for memes to spread.

Internet Age Communication

For those who have grown up with the internet, it may be difficult to imagine a time without the inescapable communications tool. People today can log on and connect with people from around the world using a computer, mobile device, television, and so much more. But there was a time when mail was delivered by hand and talking to someone in another country meant expensive long-distance phone fees.

The internet has not only changed the ways people *can* communicate, but also *how* people communicate. The internet, and social media in particular, have made it easier to maintain

Memes move easily from person to person, replicating like a virus may. It's human nature to share interesting or amusing things—both of which memes are!

friendships, live, and work. However, some believe that in an effort to bring people together, the internet has driven them further apart.

With the internet, there are now online relationships. No longer are people required to meet face-to-face or even live in the same city or country to have a relationship. Communication is conducted via any one of the available channels such as chat applications, email, or social media. Similarly, people can attend conferences online and read the news on their internet-enabled devices.[1]

Social Media

Social media is a massive part of modern communication. Facebook claims more than 1.28 billion active monthly users. On average, a person checks his or her Facebook page fourteen times a day. Each month, people watch more than 6 billion hours of video on YouTube, and on Twitter, there are around 500 million tweets a day.[2]

In a 2012 study, researchers found that social networking helped people feel like they were able to keep in touch with others even though many said they relied too much on sites such as Facebook. Many of the people in the study said that their ability to communicate with others and conflict resolution skills were not improved with social networks. Additionally, many felt that their Facebook friends were not as important as their "real" friends. Researchers found that 23 percent of their research respondents sent messages on Facebook to someone they were mad at rather than talking about it.

The research showed that most people don't believe social networking made their friendships stronger and that reliance on social networking hurts their ability to talk with others. In general, the research respondents were not convinced that social networking made a positive impact on society.[3]

Clinical psychologist Dr. Catherine Steiner-Adair believes that with so much online interaction, "There's no question kids are missing out on very critical social skills. Body language, facial expression, and . . . vocal reactions are rendered invisible." Before the internet, teenagers communicated with each other on the phone or in person. This allowed them to experiment with

A person may check Facebook up to fourteen times a day! Six billion hours of video are watched every month on YouTube, and Twitter gets 500 million tweets a day.

new social skills that teenagers today are missing out on by communicating with a screen rather than a live person.

According to the Child Mind Institute, speaking indirectly creates barriers to communication but also removes the risk required when making new friends. Dr. Steiner-Adair explains, "Part of healthy self-esteem is knowing how to say what you think and feel even when you're in disagreement with other people or it feels emotionally risky." Communicating online removes the intimidating aspects of communication. Effects of what one says are hidden behind a screen and people can keep their guards up. With chats, people can take their time responding to the other person. So it comes as no surprise when kids today say that calling someone on the phone is "too intense." The direct communication may feel too scary.[4]

Twitter

In 2006, Twitter was introduced to the world and it has had a major effect on the world and how people communicate. Information gets out to people faster than ever before. Twitter played a part in the uprisings in the Middle East, becoming a critical source of real-time news, as well as a way to raise funds for victims in crises, such as the floods in Haiti. Rumors can spread just as quickly now, too.

While Twitter gives greater access to celebrities and politicians, it also creates "thought leaders." These are people with popular accounts, who can sway the opinions of hundreds or thousands of people at one time. Similarly, no one ever needs to be alone. People tweet while watching television and have real-time conversations about their favorite shows from the comfort of behind their screens.

Twitter once restricted the length of a tweet to only 140 characters. This created a new skill in being able to simplify one's message. Twitter has since increased the character limit on tweets, but people still must be careful that what they say is not misinterpreted.[5]

Scott Fahlman is credited with creating the first smiley emoticon, in 1982! This was probably one of the first memes, given how it spread across the internet.

Early Days of Internet Memes

One of the first memes of the internet could possibly be the smiley face emoticon, which was originally typed out as ":-)". The sideways face, seen if the reader tilts his or her head to the left, was created on September 19, 1982 by Scott E. Fahlman on an early version of a discussion group on a computer network called USENET. Fahlman marked nonserious posts with his smiley emoticon, while serious posts were marked with a frowning face typed out as ":-(". The emoticons quickly spread to other communities.

In 1997, Filipino artist and designer Dino Ignacio created a website for what would become the first modern internet meme that allowed for creative freedom. The site was called Bert Is Evil and was dedicated to showing images of the Sesame Street character Bert that supposedly proved he was evil. Ignacio used image editing tools to place Bert into existing photographs such as in movie posters or famous historical events. Ignacio soon had others making similar images, and numerous different versions of the "truth about Bert" appeared online.

The website Something Awful had forums on which users spread memes. One example was the All Your Base Are Belong to Us meme that was a video of the 1989 arcade game *Zero Wing*. The game was poorly translated into English, which people found humorous. Quoting and posting images of the game reached new levels of popularity by November 2000. People used the simple and easily copied meme in new and creative ways.[6]

23

Know Your Meme

New memes emerge every day, and it's hard to keep up. The website Know Your Meme keeps a record of memes on the internet. Founded in December 2008 and currently published by Literally Media, Ltd., the site is run by an editorial and research staff with submissions from the site's users.

Know Your Meme has become an authority on all things internet meme-related. In 2014, the site was inducted into the Web Archiving Program run by the American Folklife Center at the US Library of Congress.[7]

Many more memes were created over the years that captured internet humor of the early 2000s. In 2001, Sean Connery's quote from the movie Finding Forrester, "You're the man now, dog," spawned hundreds of quotes and joke images. LOLcats, introduced in 2007 on the website 4chan, spread cat-related humor as well as the Impact font used in meme images today. One of the most popular memes was tricking others to watch the music video for Rick Astley's song "Never Gonna Give You Up." This meme, called Rickrolling, introduced the concept of trolling, or making others upset, to the mainstream.[8]

Recent Internet Memes

Memes are always evolving and changing over time. Here are just a few of the noteworthy memes in recent years.

Tardar Sauce the cat, better known to you as Grumpy Cat, spawned dozens of memes online and probably isn't done yet!

Grumpy Cat

The internet loves cats, and Grumpy Cat may be the most popular cat of all. A photo of a cat named Tardar Sauce was posted to the news aggregation website Reddit in 2012 and became a sensation. Tardar Sauce's distinct frowning face was used for an incredible number of photos with captions that conveyed feelings of dissatisfaction, annoyance, and other exaggerated negative feelings.[9]

The ALS Ice Bucket Challenge

In order to increase awareness and raise money for ALS/Lou Gehrig's disease research, the ALS Association inspired a challenge that became viral, or spread quickly across the internet. The idea was for a person to dump a bucket of water over their head, then challenge others to do the same. This stemmed from a challenge where a person was given a choice: Jump in cold water, or donate money to cancer research.

In the ice bucket challenge, some people challenged their social media followers to raise a certain amount of money for the ALS Association before the buckets were dumped. People posted videos of themselves taking the challenge on Facebook, Twitter, Instagram, and other video sharing services. Celebrities and politicians took part and the meme raised $220 million worldwide.[10]

#TheDress

In 2015, a post on the blogging and social media site Tumblr sparked a worldwide debate about colors and the science of light. The post was an image of a dress and the simple question,

"What color is this dress?" Many claimed to see a gold and white dress while others said they saw a blue and black dress. The debate was finally settled when blogs posted the science behind how light affects color perception. The dress, in the end, was blue and black.[11]

MEME EFFECT

Memes are a big part of how people communicate on the internet. Facebook posts have even expanded their capabilities to allow for animated images called GIFs to be posted instead of just text. Internet memes have even extended their replication abilities beyond the online world.

Meme Culture

Similar to how the internet changed the way people communicate, memes further changed communication between people and even created what could be considered another language. Author Cole Stryker called this "language of memes" a "visual vernacular" in which people can quickly communicate emotions and opinions. It is through this new language that people interact particularly on meme-heavy sites including YouTube, 4chan, Tumblr, 9GAG, and Reddit.[1] While each site has its own popular memes, they can transcend their origins and travel to other sites to further spread to more people.

Meme culture is seen by many as an extension of traditional cultural activities, such as storytelling and scrapbooking. With the introduction of internet technology, people are able to express themselves in a distinctly modern way. For example, the LOLCats meme shifted culture and technology into what PhD candidate Kate Miltner calls a "participatory culture." The boundaries between media consumers and producers has been blurred or eradicated. This means people have taken media into their own hands using media editing tools to create images and videos and the internet to distribute them.[2]

Memes are a huge part of how people communicate on the internet—did you share a meme with your friends this week?

Jean Burgess, professor of Digital Media and director of the Queensland University of Technology Digital Media Research Centre, agrees in the central role participation plays in video-meme culture. Burgess points out that meme-based viral videos have an "inside joke" nature to them. Once a meme-video goes mainstream, Burgess notes that it generally falls quickly out of favor. Rickrolling, which we mentioned in the previous chapter, was one such example. Once the meme was reported by the mainstream press, it lost its popularity online.[3] Once the "language of a meme" was translated to the general public, the meme lost its momentum and ability to replicate.

Not So Funny

Humor undoubtedly plays a central role in internet memes. As Burgess points out, many memes are based on a joke that has an exclusive quality. However, memes can also spread a darker tone.

In 2005, children's book author Matt Furie created a character named Pepe the Frog for his Boy's Club series on MySpace. For Furie, Pepe was a "peaceful frog-dude," who he saw as an extension of his own personality.[4] The Pepe character went on to become an internet meme used for various purposes and emotions and reactions including "Feels Good Man," "Sad Frog," and others. Pages and accounts dedicated to Pepe were created on Tumblr, Reddit, Instagram, and others. Celebrities even posted the meme, such as singer Katy Perry on November 8, 2014, tweeting out a photo to express how tired she was after traveling to Australia.[5]

Sometimes, memes go a way we'd rather they not—especially those like Pepe the Frog, who started as a harmless cartoon frog and was then appropriated by white nationalists.

The meme was eventually co-opted by the alt-right, a group of loosely connected white supremacists, neo-Nazis, and other fringe hate groups. On July 22, 2015, a version of Pepe the Frog drawn as then-presidential candidate Donald Trump was posted to 4chan. The image of Trump as Pepe gained enough popularity for Trump himself to tweet the meme on October 13, 2015.[6] In October 2016, Furie wrote in *Time* magazine that having his character used as a hate symbol was a nightmare.[7]

In September 2016, the Anti-Defamation League added Pepe to their database of hate symbols. In an attempt to reclaim the character, Furie launched a campaign to flood the internet with peaceful versions of the meme. However, the campaign was unsuccessful as the meme's new and hateful meaning was too strong to overcome. Furie eventually conceded defeat and killed the character in a one-page strip depicting his funeral surrounded by other characters from Boy's Club.[8]

Forums

Internet memes can begin anywhere online. However there are several sites notorious for their production of memes. While Facebook and Twitter are sources of memes, they are generally slower when it comes to exposing the latest memes.

Something Awful

As the number of internet users in the United States creeped to over 50 percent of the population, Richard Kyanka created the Something Awful website. The site became one of the most influential on internet humor and what many see as a meme factory. Gizmodo said Something Awful, or SA, was "indirectly responsible for almost everything amusing on the internet."[9]

The power of SA came from its discussion forums, which frequently mocked popular culture. A feature called Photoshop Friday encouraged users to create humorous images by editing photos. The practice has become commonplace online and is a big factor in how internet memes are created today.[10]

4chan

In 2003, a fifteen-year old member of the Something Awful community named Christopher "moot" Poole created his own site called 4chan. 4chan is similar to many other forums found online, except their posts or threads expire after a certain amount of time. Users are also anonymous, allowing for a culture where people will say and do whatever they want. The site has a few rules, but it is a generally chaotic place to be online.[11]

The site is a major contributor to online memes and behaviors commonplace online. Some of the memes they helped popularize include rage comics, the Chocolate Rain music video, and advice animals. Memes that begin on 4chan make it into the mainstream due to the site's users habit of posting the same content on Twitter, YouTube, and other larger platforms.[12]

4chan has been involved in several newsworthy incidents, including helping expose crimes. However, the site has also been involved in harmful events that include cyberbullying and tricking people into destroying their own property.[13]

Facebook

Facebook allows users to quickly and easily share content to people they are connected with. With a billion users, Facebook provides an easy and simple way for memes to replicate. However, despite the number of users, many of the memes on the site are older than those found on other sites.

For example, users shared a photo in 2012 of teenagers abusing a puppy, asking for their friends to help identify the people to bring them to justice. The meme spread quickly only later to be revealed that the image was quite old and the teenagers had been long since identified. Urban legends spread quickly as well, with one false story about racism on an airplane from 1998 continuing to spread on Facebook many years later.[14]

Political-themed memes are also popular on Facebook. News articles are some of the most shared items on the site. Political memes, however, do not always provide factual content and misinformation is commonplace.

Affecting Real People

While internet memes can be fun for those who participate, it can change the lives of unwilling participants. Some people become internet memes without their consent or knowledge. The surprise fame can sometimes lead to significant life changes.

One of the first internet memes was a video from 2003 that came to be known as "Star Wars Kid." The video clip involved a fourteen-year old boy named Ghyslain Raza of Quebec, Canada, enthusiastically recreating light saber fighting from

Star Wars. Some estimates place the number of views for the video at over one billion.[15]

Raza revealed in 2013 that he was the victim of bullying both over the internet and in real life because of the video. He said, "No matter how hard I tried to ignore people telling me to commit suicide, I couldn't help but feel worthless, like my life wasn't worth living." Luckily for Raza, he was able to graduate from high school and law school. He's made an effort to combat cyberbullying.[16]

Grumpy Cat

Tabatha Bundesen, owner of the cat Tardar Sauce, more popularly known as Grumpy Cat, took advantage of internet fame. She licensed her cat's likeness to be used in various products including calendars and books. There was even a Grumpy Cat movie, *Grumpy Cat's Worst Christmas Ever*.

At one point Bundesen partnered with Nick and Paul Sanford to market a line of iced coffee called Grumpy Cat Grumppuccino. According to Bundesen, the Sandfords breached their contract by creating a line of coffee grounds and T-shirts that were not part of the original agreement. After a bit of back and forth in court, Bundesen was awarded $710,000 for copyright and trademark infringement and one dollar for breach of contract.[17]

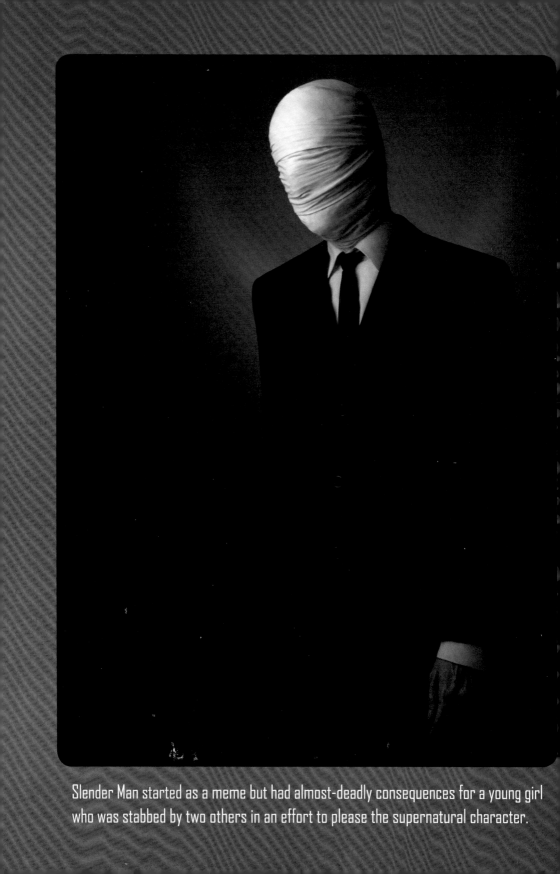

Slender Man started as a meme but had almost-deadly consequences for a young girl who was stabbed by two others in an effort to please the supernatural character.

The Something Awful forums were responsible for a meme called Slender Man. As part of a Paranormal Pictures Photoshop contest, SA user Eric Kundsen manipulated an image of children at a playground to include the ominous Slender Man figure standing in the background. Kundsen's creation would reach heights of popularity far beyond the SA forums.[18]

In 2014, two twelve-year old girls lured their friend into the woods to attack her in an attempt to please Slender Man. The two girls, Morgan Geyser and Anissa Weier, stabbed Payton Leutner multiple times before leaving her to die. Leutner was able to crawl away and get help from a bicyclist.[19]

Weier pleaded guilty and in December 2017 was sentenced to twenty-five years in a mental institution. Geyser pleaded guilty to attempted first-degree murder and, in February 2018, was committed to a mental institution for forty years.[20]

INTERNET SATIRE

Satire is not a new concept, but the internet has provided a new way to distribute it. For better or worse, more people are exposed to this unique style of humor.

What Is Satire?

Satire is an old form of comedy going back to the days of the Ancient Romans. It is used to make fun of culture, or human nature while also showing its weaknesses. Its goal is to get people to think about various problems in society and get involved with change. Satire is commonly used with other writing devices including irony, parody, and word play. Satire is similar to other forms of comedy such as mockery, cynicism, and sarcasm, and can be used with one or more.[1]

Satire was originally a literary device, meaning it was specific to the written word. However, in modern times, satire is found in any form of medium, such as television, books, cartoons, and video clips found on YouTube. Because of satire's way of pointing out the problems in society, it is frequently used in political humor. Comedians today pretend to be the same

Memes aren't a modern-day invention; their roots in satire reach back to the time of the Romans, where walls and fountains of Rome would be covered with humorous content, critiquing the politics of the day.

as those they are ridiculing. For example, comedian Stephen Colbert played a character on his Comedy Central show that was an exaggerated version of other political talk show hosts on television. Sometimes it was difficult to tell the difference between quotes from Colbert's character and real quotes from the hosts he was satirizing.

Elements of Satire

Satire is a broad term that includes various elements of comedy and literary devices. Including irony, parody, and word play, satire can also use hyperbole, sarcasm, and understatement. Irony is when someone uses words that have the opposite meaning of his or her intentions. For example, during a snowstorm someone might ironically say, "Warm outside, isn't it?" Sarcasm is similar, except with the added intent to ridicule or disrespect.

Hyperbole and understatement are opposites of one another. Hyperbole is using extreme exaggeration to emphasize a point. There are many common hyperbolic sayings including, "I'm so hungry I could eat a horse," or "Everybody knows that joke." Understatement is when someone purposefully presents something less than it really is. In the snowstorm example, an understatement might be, "Looks like a little bit of snow today."

A parody is a humorously exaggerated imitation of another person or work. Movie parodies are common on shows like *Saturday Night Live*, *The Simpsons*, or *Family Guy*. Word play is a clever use of words in a humorous way. Puns, such as "cat puns freak meowt," are an example of word play.

Limited Reach

Satire is considered successful if it points toward positive change, encourages others to think more carefully, or gain a better understanding about various topics. If satire does not do any of those things and instead provokes the behavior it disapproves of, then it can be considered a failure. Satire works because the humor is based on shared values among people.[2]

These shared values can be considered common sense. People generally understand what is right and what is wrong, and satire plays off of those common rules. However, satire is

Saturday Night Live is a weekly exploration of modern-day satire, where actors portray politicians and others, often mocking the current news cycle.

more difficult when it addresses a topic that may be viewed differently between separate people or cultures.[3]

The French satirical magazine *Charlie Hebdo* has a history of treading that line between cultures. The magazine has printed several satirical cartoons since 2006 aimed at the Islamic religion and its many followers. Many Muslims found the cartoons extremely offensive. The cartoons' intentions were lost in translation between two different cultures.

Effect on Satire

The nature of satire is to appear sincere while making what should be an obvious attempt at humor. However, satire can be so subtle as to fool people into believing that the message is genuine. With the way the internet has made sharing content with others so easy, satire gets lost among the news, memes, and thoughtful posts.

Facebook went so far as to test a satire tag that would label news stories that were not meant to be taken literally. The company said that they "received feedback that people wanted a clearer way to distinguish satirical articles from others." Users were too often fooled by humorous articles as truth, which spread misinformation. These satire articles would even fool legitimate news sources, who would quote the articles in their reporting. For example, the satire site The Daily Currant posted an article stating that former Governor of Alaska Sarah Palin was taking a job with al-Jazeera, an Arabic news company and broadcaster. Taking the satire as truth, the *Washington Post* passed on the news in one of their articles. In 2012, the *Onion*, another satire website, posted an article proclaiming Kim Jong-un, the North Korean ruler, as "the sexiest man alive." The story was then passed along by *China's People's Daily*, the official newspaper of the Chinese Communist Party.[4]

Area Mahdawi of the *Guardian* believes that because of the business model of the internet, people have become "satire-blind." Businesses make money off the internet by getting people to click on their links and visit their websites. Pages online are paid for by advertising, and advertising's goal is to get as many people as possible to see their ads and promotions. In return, content creators, such as news sites or blogs, create content to attract attention and encourage visitors to click on a link to a particular web page. This type of content is often referred to as clickbait. Internet users are then supplied with an endless stream of clickbait articles, which are meant to entertain as much as educate or inform people.[5]

Mahdawi also attributes the weakening of satire to the shorter attention spans the internet encourages in users. In 2000, the average American attention span was twelve seconds, and in 2013 it was eight seconds. A goldfish, in comparison, has the average attention span of nine seconds. Mahdawi believes that internet users are not stopping long enough to think about what they have just read. Satire requires thoughtfulness, something that is lost when people quickly scroll through pages online.[6]

Satire Today

Today, satire is dominated by political themes and stories. Comedians are finding humor in the culture of politics in the

Stephen Colbert

On October 17, 2005, Comedy Central launched *The Colbert Report* hosted by comedian Stephen Colbert.[7]

On the show, Colbert played a satirical version of himself. The character satirized conservative political talk show hosts while pointing out the failings of extreme patriotism.

The show went on to win several awards including a Primetime Emmy in the "Outstanding Variety Series" category, Emmy wins for writing, and two Peabody® Awards for Excellence in Broadcasting.[8]

The "real" Colbert is from Charleston, South Carolina. He was a member of several comedy troupes and television shows including *The Daily Show*.[9]

Steven Colbert is one of many comedians with late night shows containing segments that satirize current political events.

United States and around the world. However, nonpolitical satire is making news, too.

A "shred" video is when a video clip of a musician is edited to make it sound like the musician is playing terribly. For example, a shred video of the song "Mama Mia" by the 1970s pop group ABBA was edited with instruments out of tune and other musical mistakes. Another shred video begins with a violinist describing a Stradivarius violin, a brand of violin that is famous for being high quality. The violinist then begins playing the instrument and the audio was changed to screeching sounds and unskilled playing to comedic effect.[10]

A shred video of violinist Daniel Hope was uploaded to the internet in January 2018. One of the video's creators, Arno Lucker, intended the video as a satirical joke on Hope and the pianist he was playing with. However, Hope did not find the video funny and had his lawyers force the video off the internet. Lucker was then told that a series he presented at the prestigious Berlin Konzerthaus would not be renewed due to his shred video.[11]

Also in January 2018, a short film, *I'm Poppy*, was accepted to the Sundance Film Festival. The film stars Poppy Chan, who at first glance appears to be a young pop star with legions of fans and a popular pop album. However, Poppy Chan is a character played by Moriah Pereira and her creative partner, Titanic Sinclair, born Corey Mixter. Neither of them talk about their lives before Poppy. Poppy is always in character, speaking with a high, sweet voice that sounds strangely robotic.[12]

Due to her mysterious presentation, many debate whether Poppy is a genuine performer or a satire on internet and social media culture. Her videos have over 250 million views; her most popular, a ten-minute video of Poppy repeating "I'm Poppy," has more than 14 million views. Of her fans, Poppy says, "Oh, they're very nice. They usually ask for a selfie, which is my favorite photo to take."[13] Whether real or a satirical take on becoming a social media celebrity, Poppy is a real success.

FAKE NEWS

Politics and politicians are common targets of satire and comedians. Despite the changes in American political culture in recent years, satire has a long history with politics. However, the internet has made it more difficult to tell the difference between satirical news and real news.

Poe's Law

Ryan Milner, author of *The World Made Meme*, pointed out that in the early days of internet message boards during the 1980s, "Community guidelines would often indicate that it was hard to tell if someone was being silly or sincere." This led to the adoption of the smiley and frowning face memes, but it also led to what is now known as Poe's Law. Poe's Law was created in 2005 by a user known as "Nathan Poe" on an online creationist forum. The law states, "Without a winking smiley or other blatant display of humor, it is utterly impossible to parody a Creationist in such a way that someone won't mistake for the genuine article."[1]

This means that some people may believe that internet satire is actually true. This includes videos, articles, or images meant to be taken as humor. Satire found on a satire site may be easily seen for what it was meant to be, but once it is shared across the internet far from its original location, a satirical article loses all context.

The anonymous nature of the internet has made Poe's Law a defense against claims of offensive humor or statements. Milner says, "It's a big part of the culture of collective spaces like 4chan or Reddit, where people don't know each other interpersonally and you can't gauge intention."[2] Poe's Law has now become the defense for weaponized memes.

Donald Trump is shown as Humpty Dumpty from the nursery rhyme, atop his proposed wall for the US/Mexico border. "Humpty Dumpty sat on a wall, Humpty Dumpty had a great fall…"

For example, an online tech editor spearheaded a racist harassment campaign against actress Leslie Jones. The editor was eventually banned from Twitter, but not before he claimed that he was not being serious.[3]

Political Satire

One of the most popular types of satire is political, and it is found everywhere on the internet. Satire sites take advantage of real website addresses, changing them slightly so that the parody website might be confused for the real one. For example, the official website for the United States White House is www.whitehouse.gov, while a satire website has the address www.whitehouse.org, changing .gov for .org. Whitehouse.org contains political posters that resemble 1940s World War II posters, as well as mock speeches.[4]

Other satire sites that take advantage of misleading addresses over the years include www.bushcampaignhq.com and www.gwbush.com. These were aimed at then-Presidential candidate George W. Bush, whose campaign filed a complaint to the Federal Election Commission to have the sites taken down. The parody sites had 6.4 million page views in May 1999 while the real site for Bush's campaign, www.georgewbush.com, received only 30,000 hits in the same time period. Other candidates, including Al Gore and Steve Forbes, had their own satirical versions of their sites. There was even one for Bill Gates, who was not running for president at the time.[5] Others sites, such as the "Borowitz Report" and the *Onion*, do not play off of existing internet addresses but are satirical, too.

Politics is one of the most fertile grounds for satire and memes; satire can also take advantage of website addresses themselves, so beware where you surf.

Political satire is not just an American phenomenon. While criticizing the government varies from culture to culture, the internet has allowed people from around the world a glimpse into how political satire works in other countries.

In Germany, political satire has a long tradition in small theaters and clubs, and later television. German satire did not adapt to generational changes over the years. But with the internet, German viewers were able to view American shows and formats. The German tastes have become more "Americanized," and their satire is more playful and less serious than their earlier versions.[6]

A History of Criticism

During the 2004 US presidential election, a satirical video about the candidates accumulated millions of views on the internet. Produced by the company JibJab, the video is a streaming animation of Senator John Kerry and President George W. Bush insulting each other to the tune "This Land Is Your Land." It was a distinctly twenty-first century version of political satire, created by a company that specializes in animated comedy set to patriotic songs, which was even viewed in space by astronauts on the International Space Station.[7]

Of course, political satire did not begin in the 2000s. It can be traced back thousands of years, somewhere around 400 BCE. Benjamin Franklin was a political satirist with his 1773 work *Rules by Which a Great Empire May Be Reduced to a Small One*. Political cartoons became popular in the nineteenth century, appealing to a population that was mostly illiterate. Cartoonist Thomas Nast became famous for his political cartoons in *Harper's Weekly* magazine. Nast is credited with creating the elephant and donkey symbols for Republicans and Democrats, respectively.[8]

As movies became more commonplace, so did political satire films. Notable movies include *Dr. Strangelove or: How I Learned to Stop Worrying and Love the Bomb* (1964), *Wag the Dog* (1997), and *Bananas* (1971). Television shows joined in on political satire including *The Simpsons* and *South Park*.[9] Shows like *The Daily Show* and *The Colbert Report* brought satire to millions of cable viewers. The internet became a good resource for not only sharing clips of these movies and shows,

Benjamin Franklin was a political satirist in the 1700s; he published newspapers and chapbooks in which the greats of his day were slain with merciless humor.

but also for original videos posted online. Searching YouTube for "political satire" returns over 300,000 videos ranging from clips of Saturday Night Live to episodes of web-based shows.

The *Onion*

One of the most well-known satire sites on the internet is the *Onion*. Its satire is aimed at various politicians, celebrities, and more, often finding humor in everyday life. The site is filled with "facts" not meant to be taken as truth. Even information about itself is misleading. According to the site, the *Onion* began as a newspaper in 1756 with 4.3 trillion daily readers and is "the single most powerful and influential organization in human history." Elsewhere on the site, however, the *Onion* reveals itself as a satire site. It points out that the First Amendment protects satire as a form of free speech and expression.

The *Onion* did begin as a newspaper in 1988 in Madison, Wisconsin, founded by two college students. Some of its satirical headlines include "Cherokee Tribe Makes News As Fraction of Actress's Bloodline," "Inside: America Rates the Skin Colors. See Society, page 1D," and "U.S. Continues Quagmire-Building Effort in Afghanistan." The company moved to New York City in 2001 and eventually became a Chicago-based media company.[10]

In 2013, the *Onion* reduced its print publication and went to an online-only format. It focused its resources on creating content and videos for its website, while print versions are available in a few select cities.[11]

Fooled by Satire

On Thursday, September 29, 2011, a few seemingly alarming tweets were sent out. One read, "BREAKING: Witnesses reporting screams and gunfire heard inside Capitol building." A second read, "BREAKING: Capitol building being evacuated. 12 children held hostage by group of armed congressmen. #CongressHostage." A third tweet linked to an article title, "Congress Takes Group Of Schoolchildren Hostage."[12]

The tweets came from the *Onion*'s Twitter account, but the US Capitol Police felt it necessary to address them. Capitol Police issued a statement letting people know that conditions were normal. Sergeant Kimberly Schneider said in a press release, "There is no credibility to these stories or the twitter feeds. The US. Capitol Police are currently investigating the reporting."[13]

Social Media News

In 2017, the Pew Research Center found that 67 percent of Americans get at least some of their news from social media sources. At 45 percent of Americans, Facebook is where most people get their news followed by YouTube at 18 percent of Americans. While 74 percent of people who use Twitter get their news from tweets, it equals only 11 percent of US adults.[14]

In general, more Americans are getting their news from social media sites. They also get their news from more than one site. One quarter of US adults use two or more social media sites for news. Overall, the trend is that more people use social media as a news resource.[15] That may not be such great news in regards to separating fact from fiction.

In 2017, reporter Emma Roller tweeted about two people posing for a photo and making white power hand gestures while at the White House. What she did not know was that 4chan and other ultra-far-right media groups were engaged in an informal propaganda mission, where they tried to convince others that normal hand gestures were in fact secret white-supremacist signals. After falling for the bait, Roller was sued by Cassandra Fairbanks, one of the two people in the photo, for falsely claiming she was a white supremacist. Fairbanks claimed that the gesture was just a joke, or it was satire.[16] Social media allows jokes meant for a small audience to be broadcast out beyond the group of people who would understand its true meaning. Author Whitney Phillips says, "Now a single retweet can cause spontaneous global amplification."[17]

REAL TROUBLE

Although satire is intended to enlighten people on various topics, it does not always work as intended. Because of Poe's Law, the internet is a problematic place for satire with complicated issues to navigate.

Problems with Satire

Because satire requires a level of understanding from both the audience and the artist, satire can cause more problems than it solves. First, people may misunderstand satire. There are numerous examples of people believing satire as truth. With the speed of communication on the internet, satire can be misunderstood on a worldwide scale.

People may also misuse satire in different ways. Many label anything humorous as satire when it is not. Satire has a long history of being used to give voice to an oppressed group or to speak out against an injustice. Articles written just to entertain an provide humor, for example, are not truly satirical. Similarly, satire can be misused to further oppress a group of people or continuing injustices by discrediting victims.

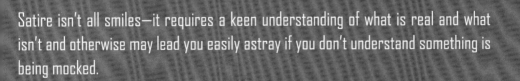

Satire isn't all smiles—it requires a keen understanding of what is real and what isn't and otherwise may lead you easily astray if you don't understand something is being mocked.

Satire has also been used as a defense. In early 2018, Dayanna Volitich, a Florida middle school social studies teacher was removed from her classroom. She secretly hosted a white supremacist podcast, and there were concerns that she exposed her students to racially charged views. Volitich released a statement that her podcast and accompanying Twitter account were works of "political satire and exaggeration."[1] A month later, however, Volitich resigned from her position.

Charlie Hebdo

Misunderstanding satire or not finding it either funny or insightful led to deadly consequences in 2015. It was then when a satirical magazine was attacked, leaving 17 people dead.[2]

Charlie Hebdo is a French magazine that began in 1970. It satirized religion and politics among other topics. In 2006, *Charlie Hebdo* reprinted cartoons that depicted the Prophet Muhammad, the founder of Islam. Many Muslims consider printing images of Muhammad as disrespectful at best and blasphemous at worst. The cartoons offended many Muslims. French President Jacques Chirac saw the decision to reprint the controversial cartoons as "overt provocation."[3]

Charlie Hebdo would not be deterred, however. The magazine published a caricature, a picture with exaggerated features, of the Prophet Muhammad in a 2011 issue. In November 2011, the *Charlie Hebdo* offices were firebombed.[4]

In 2015, January 7 to 9, two men attacked the *Charlie Hebdo* offices. There, they killed twelve people, including eight employees and a police officer. The gunmen escaped but

Charlie Hebdo, a magazine in France that dates from 1970, was the target of several terrorist attacks in the wake of its use of satirical images of the Prophet Muhammad.

were later killed after two days of terror in France. Worldwide reaction was in support of the magazine with the phrase, "Je suis Charlie," meaning "I am Charlie" becoming a rallying cry of unity. The magazine released a new edition of its magazine on January 14, just days after the attack, the cover featuring the Prophet Muhammad holding a sign reading, "Je suis Charlie."[5]

This is an example of satire not translating across different cultures. It could also be seen as satire to not respect the rules set within a group or community, in this case Muslims and Islam. Regardless, it is a prime example of the power, and danger, of satire.

Twitter Versus Germany

Beatrix von Storch, an outspoken member of the right-wing German political party Alternative for Germany, made offensive statements about Muslims and Islamic men on Twitter. *Titanic*, a satire magazine based in Germany, posted a series of tweets on January 2, 2018, satirizing von Storch. Its tweets were supposedly from von Storch and repeated her offensive statements in an attempt to be humorous. Twitter blocked von Storch's account but also blocked *Titanic*'s account.[6]

Germany has some of the toughest laws in the world on defamation, threats of violence, and urging people to commit crimes. A new law was put into effect on January 1, 2018, which enables the government to impose fines of up to 50 million euros, or about $60 million, on social media companies that do not quickly remove hate speech from their sites. There have been protests against the new law from different groups including a national journalists association that claims the law violates free speech. The Association of German Journalists (DJV) said the law was a form of censorship.[7]

Titanic was shocked by the the fine and blocking of its Twitter account. *Titanic*'s chief editor, Tim Wolff, was concerned with the law undermining satire. However, after forty-eight hours of suspension its account was back online. In a response in line with the satirical magazine's humor, Wolff said he was thankful for Twitter handling the issue "so bureaucratically and slowly," and that *Titanic* was happy for "the chance to take Twitter to task from our own account."[8]

Putin's Absence

Russian president Vladimir Putin is a common figure in the state-run media. However, for one week in March 2015, he was noticeably absent from the public's view. The government insisted that he was fine and that the government was running normally. They even shared video of Putin working at his home.[9]

However, this did not stop a wave of satire mocking Putin's absence. Ukrainian children created a cartoon showing the Russian leader being abducted by aliens, while a YouTube video showed men walking past Putin's gravestone. The amount of humor at Putin's expense did not please the government. His spokesman said, "Yes. We've already said this a hundred times. This isn't funny any more."[10]

In this case, satire was apparently a solid defense for *Titanic*'s Twitter account. Although the matter was not resolved at a speed acceptable to the magazine, a careful look into the offending tweets' source cleared up any potential misunderstandings. The tweets were legitimately satirical in nature, and for now, free speech won out.

Chinese Resistance

China has a reputation of maintaining total control over its citizens' communications on the internet, China is an

Even Russian president Vladimir Putin became the target of satire and memes when he went "missing" in the spring of 2015.

authoritarian country that enforces strict obedience to the government at the cost of the personal freedom of the people who live there. One example is how the country's government extensively filters websites and web content, particularly when it involves political topics.

Combined with the use of satire to shed light on problems in the world, the internet could be a powerful tool for the people of China. It might explain why internet satire has thrived in China. Online parody in particular is a part of Chinese popular culture.[11]

One of the first examples came about after a news report about internet video services and the urgent need to purify the internet aired on China Central Television Station (CCTV). In it, a thirteen-year-old girl called web content she viewed as "very yellow and very violent." The word "yellow" is used in China to describe something as vulgar. Soon, caricatures of the girl and the news report circulated Chinese internet spaces. The caricatures questioned the validity of the news report. Many believed that the girl was coached into saying that internet videos were violent. Other forms of satire took the form of stories, jokes, blog posts, fake biographies of the girl from the news report, and more.[12]

In the end, Chinese citizens protested a government they believed was spreading propaganda through the state-run news channel. Internet satire became the medium of protest. The term "VYVV," an initialism for "very yellow very violent," became a widely used term in China. People began to consider CCTV as a "fake news" network. CCTV and the authorities were subject to public ridicule for a period of time. As time went on, the VYVV movement died down, but its legacy remains.[13]

Spreading Lies

When users log into Facebook, they are met with a news feed of stories posted by their friends, family, and by Facebook itself. With a series of news stories at hand, people may mistake a satirical story for a real one. As the satirical story spreads, its original meaning is lost. Suddenly, the "fake news" is taken as real, leaving many in confusion over what is and is not true.

This exact scenario happened with the satirical news site Real News Right Now. The site's author created a headline about the United States housing 250,000 Syrian refugees at Navajo, Standing Rock Indian Reservations. The author, who chose to remain anonymous, thought that his headline sounded too ridiculous to be taken seriously. However, Fox News's Sean Hannity began repeating the headline, which was then spread further when then-presidential candidate Donald Trump quoted the headline in interviews.[14]

Facebook has spent years trying to fix the issue with misleading information spreading via its site. They have identified three types of sources of false stories including foreign government interference, automated programs called bots, and legitimate news sources with low levels of accuracy and trustworthiness. However, satirical sources are a separate category, since people may share the story without realizing their mistake. To combat this, Facebook introduced an "information icon." When a news story appears on a user's newsfeed, Facebook includes a clickable letter "i" that provides information on the news source. The hope is that people will click and learn if the story they are seeing is meant as humor or to be taken seriously. The feature went live for the United States on April 4, 2018.[15]

Step Away from the Tide Pods

A key to internet memes and satire is moderation and checking your sources to know what you're reading. Memes evolve daily and even hourly, so to keep your cats ungrumpy, and your ricks rolling, definitely step away from the Tide Pods—unless you're doing laundry.

CHAPTER NOTES

Introduction

1. Alina Selyukh, "Teenagers Are Still Eating Tide Pods, but Don't Expect a Product Redesign," NPR, January 30, 2018, https://www.npr.org/2018/01/30/581925549/teenagers-are-still-eating-tide-pods-but-dont-expect-a-product-redesign.
2. *Onion*, "Tide Debuts New Sour Apple Detergent Pods," July 11, 2017, https://www.theonion.com/tide-debuts-new-sour-apple-detergent-pods-1819580060.
3. Selyukh, "Teenagers Are Still Eating Tide Pods, but Don't Expect a Product Redesign."
4. Lindsey Bever, "Teens Are Daring Each Other to Eat Tide Pods. We Don't Need to Tell You That's a Bad Idea," *Washington Post*, January 17, 2018, https://www.washingtonpost.com/news/to-your-health/wp/2018/01/13/teens-are-daring-each-other-to-eat-tide-pods-we-dont-need-to-tell-you-thats-a-bad-idea/?utm_term=.b2277bc6046c.
5. Ibid.
6. Claire McCarthy, MD, "Why Teenagers Eat Tide pods," Harvard Health Blog, January 30, 2018, https://www.health.harvard.edu/blog/why-teenagers-eat-tide-pods-2018013013241.
7. Ibid.

Chapter 1
The Selfish Meme

1. Richard Dawkins, *The Selfish Gene* (Oxford, UK: Oxford University Press, 1976).
2. Ibid.
3. Richard Brodie, *Virus of the Mind: the New Science of the Meme* (London, UK: Hay House, 2009).
4. BBC News, "Profile: Richard Dawkins," BBC News, September 07, 2012, http://www.bbc.co.uk/religion/0/19177976.
5. James Gleick, "What Defines a Meme?" Smithsonian.com, May 01, 2011, https://www.smithsonianmag.com/arts-culture/what-defines-a-meme-1904778.
6. Ibid.
7. Ibid.
8. Ibid.
9. Ibid.
10. Dawkins, *The Selfish Gene*, p. 192.
11. Dawkins, *The Selfish Gene*, p. 194.
12. Ibid.
13. Dawkins, *The Selfish Gene*, p. 19.
14. Gleick, "What Defines a Meme?"
15. Ibid.

Chapter 2
Memes on the Internet

1. Pimenov Maxim, "Public Access—How Internet Changed the Way We Communicate," Engadget, November 29, 2016, https://www.engadget.com/2016/11/29/how-internet-changed-the-way-we-communicate.

2. Willy Kruh, "Social Media Have Changed How We Communicate Ideas," *Globe and Mail*, March 25, 2017, https://www.theglobeandmail.com/report-on-business/careers/careers-leadership/social-media-have-changed-how-we-communicate-ideas/article19385666.

3. John Drussell, "Social Networking and Interpersonal Communication and Conflict Resolution Skills among College Freshmen" (2012), *Master of Social Work Clinical Research Papers*, Paper 21, http://sophia.stkate.edu/msw_papers/21.

4. Rachel Ehmke, "How Using Social Media Affects Teenagers," Child Mind Institute, https://childmind.org/article/how-using-social-media-affects-teenagers.

5. Doug Gross, "5 Ways Twitter Changed How We Communicate," CNN, March 21, 2011, http://www.cnn.com/2011/TECH/social.media/03/21/twitter.birthday.communication/index.html.

6. Linda Börzsei, "Makes a Meme Instead: A Concise History of Internet Memes." *New Media Studies Magazine 7*, http://www.academia.edu/3649116/Makes_a_Meme_Instead_A_Concise_History_of_Internet_Memes.

7. "About Know Your Meme," Know Your Meme, http://knowyourmeme.com/about.

8. Ben Huh, "10 Classic Memes That Owned the Internet," CNN, March 12, 2014, http://www.cnn.com/2014/03/11/opinion/10-classic-internet-memes/index.html.

9. Elise Moreau, "The Top 10 Most Popular Memes of All Time," Lifewire, https://www.lifewire.com/top-memes-of-all-time-3485903.

10. Ibid.

11. Ibid.

Chapter 3
Meme Effect

1. Kate Miltner, "'There's No Place for Lulz on LOLCats': The Role of Genre, Gender, and Group Identity in the Interpretation and Enjoyment of an Internet Meme." *First Monday* 19, no. 8 (2014).
2. Ibid.
3. Jean Burgess, "'All Your Chocolate Rain Are Belong To Us?' Viral Video, You Tube and the Dynamics of Participatory Culture." *In Art in the Global Present* (UTSePress, 2014), pp. 86–96.
4. Elle Hunt, "Pepe the Frog Creator Kills Off Internet Meme Co-opted by White Supremacists," *Guardian*, May 07, 2017, https://www.theguardian.com/world/2017/may/08/pepe-the-frog-creator-kills-off-internet-meme-co-opted-by-white-supremacists.
5. "Pepe the Frog," Know Your Meme, February 04, 2018, http://knowyourmeme.com/memes/pepe-the-frog.
6. Ibid.
7. Elle Hunt, "Pepe the Frog Creator Kills Off Internet Meme Co-opted by White Supremacists."
8. Ibid.
9. David Britton, "How Something Awful Taught the Internet How to Laugh at Itself," Daily Dot, November 05, 2017, https://www.dailydot.com/unclick/something-awful-history.
10. Ibid.
11. Caitlin Dewey. "Absolutely Everything You Need to Know to Understand 4chan, the Internet's Own Bogeyman," *Washington Post*, September 25, 2014, https://www.washingtonpost.com/news/the-intersect/wp/2014/09/25/absolutely-everything-you-need-to-know-to-understand-4chan-the-internets-own-bogeyman/?utm_term=.5a8f49aae3ae.

12. Ibid.

13. Ibid.

14. Suzanne Choney, "The Ugly Dark Side of Facebook Memes," TODAY.com, April 21, 2012, https://www.today.com/money/ugly-dark-side-facebook-memes-727490.

15. Rebecca Hawkes, "Whatever Happened to Star Wars Kid? The Sad but Inspiring Story Behind One of the First Victims of Cyberbullying," *Telegraph*, May 04, 2016, http://www.telegraph.co.uk/films/2016/05/04/whatever-happened-to-star-wars-kid-the-true-story-behind-one-of.

16. Ibid.

17. Scott Neuman, "Grumpy Cat Awarded $710,000 in Copyright Infringement Suit," NPR, January 25, 2018, https://www.npr.org/sections/thetwo-way/2018/01/25/580588088/grumpy-cat-awarded-710-000-in-copyright-infringement-suit.

18. David Britton, "How Something Awful Taught the Internet How to Laugh at Itself."

19. Scott Neuman, "Wisconsin Teen Sentenced to 40 Years in Mental Hospital for Slender Man Stabbing," NPR, February 02, 2018, https://www.npr.org/sections/thetwo-way/2018/02/02/582618068/wisconsin-teen-sentenced-to-40-years-in-mental-hospital-for-slender-man-stabbing.

20. Ibid.

Chapter 4

Internet Satire

1. Sophia A. McClennen and Remy M. Maisel, *Is Satire Saving Our Nation?: Mockery and American Politics* (New York, NY: Palgrave Macmillan, 2014).

2. Tim Parks, "The Limits of Satire," *New York Review of Books*, January 16, 2015, http://www.nybooks.com/daily/2015/01/16/charlie-hebdo-limits-satire.

3. Ibid.

4. Arwa Mahdawi, "Satire Is Dying Because the Internet Is Killing It," *Guardian*, August 19, 2014, https://www.theguardian.com/commentisfree/2014/aug/19/satire-tag-internet-killing-facebook-tag.

5. Ibid.

6. Ibid.

7. "Stephen Colbert Bio," Comedy Central Press, http://press.cc.com/series/the-colbert-report/bio/69253.

8. Ibid.

9. Ibid.

10. Michael Cooper, "Can Classical Music Take a Joke? A Violinist Is Shredded," *New York Times*, January 19, 2018, https://www.nytimes.com/2018/01/19/arts/music/daniel-hope-violin-deutsche-grammophon-shredding.html.

11. Ibid.

12. Scott D. Pierce, "She's Poppy—and She's Coming to Sundance with her New YouTube Red Series About a Jealous Mannequin and a Deal with the Devil," *Salt Lake Tribune*, January 23, 2018. https://www.sltrib.com/news/2018/01/23/shes-poppy-and-shes-coming-to-sundance-with-her-new-youtube-red-series-about-jealous-mannequins-and-deals-with-the-devil.

13. Ibid.

Chapter 5
Fake News

1. Emma Grey Ellis, "Can't Take a Joke? That's Just Poe's Law, 2017's Most Important Internet Phenomenon," *Wired*, June 07, 2017, https://www.wired.com/2017/06/poes-law-troll-cultures-central-rule.
2. Ibid.
3. Ibid.
4. Mark Stoner and Sally Perkins, *Making Sense of Messages: a Critical Apprenticeship in Rhetorical Criticism* (Abingdon, UK: Routledge, 2016).
5. Anne P. Mintz, *Web of Deception: Misinformation on the Internet*, Paw Prints, 2008.
6. Geoffrey Baym and Jeffrey P. Jones, *News Parody and Political Satire Across the Globe* (Abingdon, UK: Routledge, 2017).
7. Sue Marquette Poremba, "Probing Question: How Old Is political satire?" Penn State University, June 20, 2008, http://news.psu.edu/story/141311/2008/06/20/research/probing-question-how-old-political-satire.
8. Ibid.
9. Ibid.
10. Eric Konigsberg, "Collecting Headlines Funnier Than This," *New York Times*, November 2, 2009, http://www.nytimes.com/2009/11/03/books/03onion.html.
11. Roger Yu, "The Onion Ends Print Publication After 25 years," *USA Today*, November 08, 2013, https://www.usatoday.com/story/money/business/2013/11/08/the-onion-ends-print/3475217.

12. David Marino-Nachison, "Capitol Police Issue 'All Clear' Following Onion Tweets, Article," *Washington Post*, September 29, 2011, https://www.washingtonpost.com/blogs/crime-scene/post/capitol-police-issue-all-clear-following-onion-tweets-article/2011/09/29/gIQAYs4J7K_blog.html?utm_term=.2f0fd971922c.

13. Ibid.

14. Elisa Shearer and Jeffrey Gottfried, "News Use Across Social Media Platforms 2017," Pew Research Center's Journalism Project, September 07, 2017, http://www.journalism.org/2017/09/07/news-use-across-social-media-platforms-2017.

15. Ibid.

16. Emma Grey Ellis, "Can't Take a Joke? That's Just Poe's Law, 2017's Most Important Internet Phenomenon."

17. Ibid.

Chapter 6
Real Trouble

1. Phil McCausland and Erik Ortiz, "Reading, Writing and Racism? Florida Teacher Hosted White Nationalist Podcast," NBCNews.com, March 5, 2018, https://www.nbcnews.com/news/us-news/florida-school-removes-teacher-who-hosted-white-nationalist-podcast-n853096.

2. "2015 Charlie Hebdo Attacks Fast Facts," CNN, December 25, 2017, https://www.cnn.com/2015/01/21/europe/2015-paris-terror-attacks-fast-facts/index.html.

3. Ibid.

4. Ibid.

5. Ibid.

6. Emma Thomasson, "German Hate Speech Law Tested as Twitter Blocks Satire Account," Reuters, January 3, 2018, https://www.reuters.com/article/us-germany-hatecrime/german-hate-speech-law-tested-as-twitter-blocks-satire-account-idUSKBN1ES1AT.

7. Ibid.

8. David Martin, "German Satire Magazine Titanic Back on Twitter Following 'Hate Speech' Ban," DW.COM, January 6, 2018, http://www.dw.com/en/german-satire-magazine-titanic-back-on-twitter-following-hate-speech-ban/a-42046485.

9. Reuters, "Putin's Absence Inspires Online Satire and Rumors of Death," Newsweek, March 21, 2016, http://www.newsweek.com/putins-absence-inspires-online-satire-and-rumors-death-313856.

10. Ibid.

11. Lijun Tang and Syamantak Bhattacharya, "Power and Resistance: A Case Study of Satire on the Internet," Sociological Research Online 16(2)11.

12. Ibid.

13. Ibid.

14. Rachel Kaser, "Facebook Update Shows Which of Your Friends Are Suckers for Fake News," The Next Web, April 03, 2018, https://thenextweb.com/facebook/2018/04/04/facebook-update-shows-friends-suckers-fake-news.

15. Ibid.

GLOSSARY

authoritarian Enforcing strict obedience to the government in exchange for personal freedoms.

blasphemous Disrespectful toward God or sacred things.

clickbait Content created to draw attention and encourage visitors to click on a link.

co-opt To adopt an idea for one's own use.

emoticon A facial expression represented by forming various combinations of keyboard characters.

evolution The process by which different kinds of living organisms are thought to have developed and diversified from earlier forms during the history of the earth.

exclusive Something restricted or limited to a specific group or people.

hyperbole Extreme exaggeration used to emphasize a point.

irony The use of words that mean the opposite of what one intends.

parody A humorously exaggerated imitation.

propagate To spread and promote an idea or theory.

replicate To make an exact copy of or reproduce.

satire Something meant to make fun of and show the weaknesses of human nature or a particular person.

trolling To make a deliberately offensive or provocative post to upset someone and make them angry.

viral An image, video, or other digital media that is circulated quickly on the internet.

FURTHER READING

Books

Chess, Shira, and Eric Newsom. *Folklore, Horror Stories, and the Slender Man the Development of an Internet Mythology*. Basingstoke, UK: Palgrave Macmillan, 2015.

Kavanaugh, Beatrice. *Computing and the Internet*. Broomall, PA: Mason Crest, 2017.

Roberts, Kathryn. *The Fifth Estate: Extreme Viewpoints from Alternative Media*. New York, NY: Greenhaven Publishing, 2018.

Shifman, Limor. *Memes in Digital Culture*. Cambridge, MA: MIT Press, 2014.

Websites

DigitalGov
www.digitalgov.gov
DigitalGov is a website run by the US government that provides tools and information to help people create digital services including GIFs and memes.

FactCheck.org
www.factcheck.org
The FactCheck.org project is a nonpartisan service that monitors the factual accuracy in political news stories.

INDEX